DAVID
BOWIE
ever changing hero

Publisher and Creative Director: Nick Wells

Project Editor: Polly Prior

Art Director: Mike Spender

Layout Design: Jane Ashley

Digital Design and Production: Chris Herbert

Special thanks to: Frances Bodiam, Laura Bulbeck, Emma Chafer, Esme Chapman,
Karen Fitzpatrick, Daniela Nava

FLAME TREE PUBLISHING

Crabtree Hall, Crabtree Lane

Fulham, London SW6 6TY

United Kingdom

www.flametreepublishing.com

www.flametreemusic.com

First published 2013

14 16 17 15 13

1 3 5 7 9 10 8 6 4 2

A CIP record for this book is available from the British Library upon request.

ISBN 978-0-85775-989-4

Printed in China

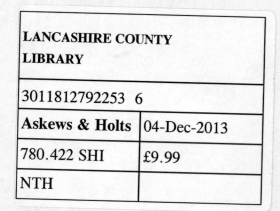

DAVID
BOWIE
ever changing hero

SEAN EGAN

Foreword: Malcolm Mackenzie

**FLAME TREE
PUBLISHING**

CONTENTS

FOREWORD

Ziggy Stardust and the Spiders From Mars was released the year I was born. Songs like 'Changes' and 'Starman' were as familiar as 'The Wheels On The Bus', and 'Let's Dance' and 'Modern Love' sound-tracked my school discos, but it wasn't until a chance encounter with *Hunky Dory* at 14, that I was confronted with the enigmatic genius of the former David Jones. I heard 'Life On Mars' and it was an Aladdin Sane lightning flash to the frontal cortex. Bowie had contacted me through space, time and black plastic. I was dumbfounded by its otherworldly beauty and moved to tears.

The music shook me, but the man, or perhaps the myth, the hair and Freddie Buretti lapels sealed the obsession. The wild-eyed boy from Bromley took me on a fantastic voyage through post-apocalyptic dystopias ruled by diamond dogs, alien rock gods and addict Pierrot spacemen. He guided me into the underground of New York's gay scene and out of the underground of Goblin King Jareth – even when Bowie lost his way in the labyrinth of the 1980s he was still amazing.

His impact on popular culture has been inestimable, but frankly it's still not enough. Every pop star should ask themselves: 'what would David Bowie do?' Good luck answering that. Instinct, genius and charisma cannot easily be devoured and regurgitated; though it has been fun watching artists like Lady Gaga try.

This year Bowie seemed to become the enigmatic Nikola Tesla he played in Christopher Nolan's film *The Prestige* – producing an album out of a hat – after 10 years of silence, that just happens to coincide with a record-breaking retrospective at the V&A. Ahhhhhhhh, wham-bam thank you ma'am!

Hunky Dory is still my favourite Bowie LP, but *Ziggy*, *Low* and *Diamond Dogs* come close, then there's *"Heroes"*, *1.Outside*, *Lodger* and *The Next Day*, which is shaping up to be the best album of 2013 … not bad going for a funny old kook with 50 years in the business.

Malcolm Mackenzie

Editor, *We Love Pop*

TAKE A BOW

'IF ANYTHING
MAYBE I'VE
HELPED
ESTABLISH THAT
ROCK'N'ROLL
I SUPPOSE.'
DAVID BOWIE,
1975

Young mod. Hairy hippie. Ziggy Stardust. Aladdin Sane. Halloween Jack. The Thin White Duke. Plastic Soulman. Godfather of the New Romantics. Tin Machinist.

Across the course of his four decades-plus career, David Bowie has adopted more personas and musical genres than just about any other musical icon. He has viewed his music and public profile as intertwined, at one point having a different image for each new album. By wrapping himself in artifice, he not only brought to pop a new theatricality but he also kept the world intrigued and waiting for the next instalment of his glittering career.

Not Just A Pretty Face

Sometimes lost in all of this was the fact of Bowie's vast musical talents. Throughout the 1970s, at a point where many people had assumed rock had been taken as far as it could go, he broadened the medium's parameters with a sequence of ground-breaking albums. *The Man Who Sold The World* (1970) was that contradiction: intellectual heavy metal. *Hunky Dory* (1971) was a jaw-droppingly skilful and diverse display of alternative songwriting. *Ziggy Stardust* (1972) was a blatant tilt for mainstream success whose cynicism could not blunt its brilliance. *Aladdin Sane* (1973) spat in the face of his new teen idol status with profanities, sexual explicitness and discordant piano. *Young Americans* (1975) saw him become a soul man, although his soul was typically of a deliberately arch style. *Station to Station* (1976) found him taking pop into epic, elegant pastures. Then there was the Berlin Trilogy of *Low* (1977), *"Heroes"* (1977) and *Lodger* (1979), in which he spurned anything resembling the commercial with electronic and ambient experimentalism.

The artistic trajectory described here was a rollercoaster ride, the type of which is rarely embarked upon by recording artists because, by definition, comprehensively overhauling your sound runs the risk of turning off your original fans. Bowie caused his devotees to confront their reasons for buying his product over and over again. Each time, he emerged unscathed – indeed, triumphant – as his fanbase learned to love and expect his reinventions.

'I GOT INTO ROCK BECAUSE IT WAS AN ENJOYABLE WAY OF MAKING MY MONEY AND TAKING FOUR OR FIVE YEARS TO PUZZLE THE NEXT MOVE OUT.'

DAVID BOWIE

Low Points

This is not to say that Bowie has not had career troughs. His surrendering to fashionable empty gloss on *Let's Dance* (1983) and *Tonight* (1984) in the Eighties was financially savvy but lost him fans who could forgive any career direction except pedestrianism. Meanwhile, his sublimation of himself into the group Tin Machine in the late Eighties/early Nineties was an act of self-sacrifice and daring rendered pointless by the ensemble's mediocrity.

Yet, ever the contrarian, Bowie refused to let this become the narrative of the long artistic decline of the likes of The Who or The Rolling Stones: at a point where many had given up on him, he hauled himself back to artistic credibility with a series of albums that showed that he alone of his generation of artists was interested in embracing musical forms that had not existed when he made his first record.

Back With A Bang

It was because of this that the announcement in 2013 of *The Next Day* – his first new album in 10 years – was greeted not with a 'so what?' but instead with genuine excitement. True to form, Bowie did not let anyone down when it came either to intriguing imagery, playing cat and mouse with the media or artistic worth.

His reappearance made anyone who had forgotten, or been given cause for doubt, realize all over again that David Bowie is truly a unique star in the musical firmament.

'I'M GOING TO BE HUGE AND IT'S QUITE FRIGHTENING IN A WAY BECAUSE I KNOW THAT WHEN ... IT'S TIME FOR ME TO BE BROUGHT DOWN, IT WILL BE WITH A BUMP!'

DAVID BOWIE, 1971

DAVID JONES

As is the case with pretty much all stars, before the beautiful butterfly came the unremarkable caterpillar.

Bowie was born not on Mars but in Brixton, South London. He started life as David Robert Jones on 8 January 1947. His father was a promotions officer for the children's charity Barnardo's and his mother a cinema usherette. He had one sibling – half-brother Terry – who had, like much of the extended family, severe mental problems. By the time Bowie was six, the family had moved to Bromley in Kent.

School Up And Downs

Although he was precocious at the recorder and school mime lessons, young Jones was not so academically gifted as to

pass the old eleven-plus exam. Aged fifteen, while he was at Bromley Technical High School, he got into a fight with one George Underwood over a girl. A facial punch saw Jones hospitalized for several months with what eventually turned out to be a permanently injured eye. The consequent dilation of its pupil gives the illusion in photographs of it being a different colour to his other eye. This surreal sight aided his attempt to portray himself as an extra-terrestrial rocker in the early Seventies. Amazingly, Jones and Underwood remained friendly, with the latter designing the artwork for early Bowie albums.

Another fellow alumnus of Bromley Technical High School was Peter Frampton, who credits Jones with setting him on the path to his own rock stardom – originally far greater than Bowie's – via encouragement and informal lessons. Bowie would later help him again, recruiting him to tour in the Eighties when Frampton's star had waned.

Convert To Rock

As had been the case with a vast swathe of his generation, David Jones was instantly converted to the status of True Believer in Rock 'N' Roll by the excitement of hearing the first wave of rock heroes – in his case particularly Elvis, Little Richard and Fats Domino. Britain duly bequeathed a wave of its own rock heroes, thanks to a musical do-it-yourself craze for skiffle. Bowie was no exception to this fashion for taking up a makeshift instrument with a group of mates. He soon graduated from tea-chest bass to proper instruments, dabbling in several but becoming adept at guitar and saxophone.

'MY BROTHER TERRY'S IN AN ASYLUM RIGHT NOW. I'D LIKE TO BELIEVE THAT THE INSANITY IS BECAUSE OUR FAMILY ALL GENIUS, BUT I'M AFRAID THAT'S NOT TRUE.'

Bowie was in musical groups called The Konrads, The King Bees, The Manish Boys and The Lower Third. Some of them got music press notices and others even record releases but none lasted long. It was always Jones who caught the eye: a good-looking young peacock and would-be polymath (even then he was publicly talking about a desire to act).

What's In A Name?

Somewhere in all this, Jones became Bowie to avoid confusion with a contemporary thespian called David Jones, better known as Davy Jones of The Monkees. The *nom de guerre* was taken from Jim Bowie, legendary American frontiersman who died at the battle of the Alamo and gave his name to the formidable-looking Bowie knife. The adopted name's intended connotations of muscular derring-do were rather wasted in America, where the word is pronounced in a rather more camp way: 'Boo-ee'.

By 1967 Bowie had graduated to the solo career that was perhaps always inevitable for a man of such singular vision. His first record was the whimsical 'The Laughing Gnome', a tale of being stalked by a little person with a laughing-gas voice. Was this a clear precursor to a life of prodigious achievement? Hardly. It was terrible.

'IT'S ODD BUT EVEN WHEN I WAS A KID, I WOULD WRITE ABOUT "OLD AND OTHER TIMES" AS THOUGH I HAD A LOT OF YEARS BEHIND ME.'

DAVID BOWIE

WHO DOES HE LOVE?

'WHEN I HEARD LITTLE RICHARD, I MEAN, IT JUST SET MY WORLD ON FIRE.'
DAVID BOWIE

David Bowie has inspired more musicians than most recording artists, but he naturally also had his own formative influences.

It almost goes without saying that Elvis Presley was important to him: few of the musicians who became teenagers in the Sixties weren't overwhelmed by The King's stunning larynx and greaseball beauty. Perhaps revealingly, Bowie – a man who has often appeared to be as much into music's effect as its content – seemed mostly impressed by Elvis's impact on people, him marvelling in an interview about an incident where a cousin got up and launched into an abandoned dance to the strains of 'Hound Dog'.

Little Richard To Jazz

Another revealing detail, perhaps, is Bowie's love for Little Richard. The piano-pounder with a towering pompadour and Errol Flynn moustache had an outrageous, androgynous image and laced his lyrics with sexual explicitness that the grown-ups were too square to understand. Remind you of anyone?

Almost predictably, though, Bowie's love of music was more nuanced than that of his peers. He was turned on to modern jazz by his brother, leading to the 'difficult' likes of Charles Mingus and John Coltrane often inhabiting the family turntable. Jazz's penchant for wandering time signatures and elastic form can be discerned in Bowie's more experimental works, while the alto sax, which his love of the genre inspired him to take up, can be heard scattered throughout his entire catalogue.

Marc Bolan

Bowie's first album speaks of a love of the studiedly English singer Anthony Newley, while *Hunky Dory* featured 'Song for Bob Dylan', in which he lamented Dylan's current loss of form. Although most would claim that Marc Bolan was a musical pygmy compared to Bowie's goliath, it cannot be denied that the T. Rex man was more than just a mate. The glam rock movement that Bolan kicked off with his glittered cheeks and feather boas made possible the more sophisticated ventures by Bowie into that foppish territory. It's rumoured that Bowie's 'Lady Stardust' is at least partly about Bolan.

'HE WAS A MAJOR HERO OF MINE. AND I WAS PROBABLY STUPID ENOUGH TO BELIEVE THAT HAVING THE SAME BIRTHDAY AS HIM ACTUALLY MEANT SOMETHING.'

DAVID BOWIE ON ELVIS

Producing His Idols

One of Bowie's most enduring influences was The Velvet Underground. This New York-based ensemble had no hits and little success during their 1967–70 recording career but, in writing gritty songs about street life, drug addiction and violence, helped popular music to grow up. This growing process applied to their sonics as much as their lyrics: they experimented with atonality, dissonance and extemporization, even while insisting on their right to purvey pretty melody. Bowie acknowledged on the sleeve of *Hunky Dory* that that album's buzzsaw rocker 'Queen Bitch' was a Velvet Underground pastiche. Bowie repaid his artistic debt to the band by producing with Mick Ronson *Transformer*, the 1972 album by Lou Reed (frontman and chief songwriter of the Velvets) which bequeathed UK hit single 'Walk On The Wild Side'.

In fact, Bowie's early Seventies production work is a veritable litmus test of his respect for specific artists. He also offered a helping studio hand to The Stooges – pioneering punk-metallers coming to the end of their tumultuous life – and their frontman Iggy Pop, who was just beginning his solo career. In Mott the Hoople he actually rescued an admired band, who had decided to split up, and set them on the path to greater glory by gifting them a hit with 'All The Young Dudes' and helming their 1972 album of the same name. He then watched them achieve even greater success after their frontman Ian Hunter elected to base his new songwriting technique on 'Dudes" pop culture iconography.

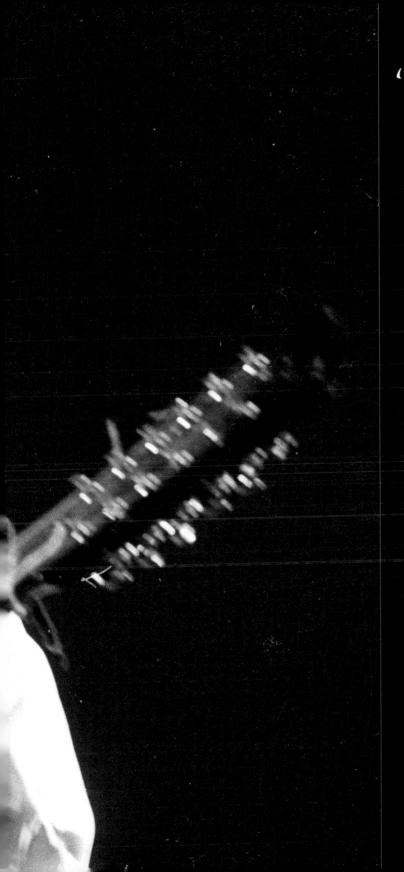

'THE FEW TIMES I SAW HIM PERFORM IN LONDON... DURING THE '60s WILL FOREVER BE ETCHED IN MY MIND.'

DAVID BOWIE ON SYD BARRETT

DAVID BOWIE

'I DID A LOT
OF NEWLEY
THINGS ON
THE VERY FIRST
ALBUM I MADE
... THAT'S A
VERY STRANGE
ALBUM.'
DAVID BOWIE

Bowie's eponymous debut album appeared in June 1967. *David Bowie* was the work of a man who didn't yet know quite what to do with his talent.

There was baroque pop, northern brass band music and music hall numbers – all with melodies that were pretty enough but somehow just this side of memorable. The instrumentation was the sort of stuff fashionable in a year where the young took delight in co-opting the traditional for their own ends (e.g. hip kids dressing in old military uniforms) but there's only so many parping horns and pom-pom-pom drums that one can take, and they form part of an overarching, self-conscious whimsy that is a little suffocating. The lyrics inevitably drip with Bowie's intelligence and inquisitive eye but the character studies on offer aren't exactly 'Eleanor Rigby'. However, although there are no Bowie

'IT WAS VERY WEIRD. MY FATHER DIED AND A WEEK LATER I HAD A HIT RECORD.'

DAVID BOWIE ON 'SPACE ODDITY'

classics present, there are a clutch of songs that point to the fact that this is a man with a future if he can only harness his inchoate abilities.

The Arts Lab

While resident in the South London suburb of Beckenham in 1969, Bowie, along with three friends, set up a folk club at the pub The Three Tuns. This developed into the Beckenham Arts Laboratory. Although many eventually famous rockers played there – including Peter Frampton, Steve Harley, The Strawbs, Rick Wakeman and Mick Ronson – the 'Arts Lab' was also a reflection of how multi-faceted Bowie's interests were: there was painting, poetry readings, light shows, street theatre, dance and puppetry in this crucible of nascent talent. Some of Bowie's ex-associates – ones admittedly likely to be disdainful of pop music – will tell you that it's the best thing with which he's ever been involved. He was certainly far more interested in the Arts Lab than making a second album for quite a while.

The Difficult Second Album

Bowie's second album was a bit better than the first but mainly lifted beyond the status of 'Mediocre Follow-up to Mediocre Debut' by one of its tracks being released beforehand as a single and becoming a smash hit and thence a staple of oldies radio.

'A LOT OF THE MAN WHO SOLD THE WORLD WOULD HAVE BEEN BETTER IF I'D DONE IT LATER.'

DAVID BOWIE

'I STILL DON'T CONSIDER MYSELF A PERFORMER. I'M A WRITER. I REALLY WOULDN'T LIKE TO MAKE SINGING A FULL-TIME OCCUPATION.'

DAVID BOWIE, 1969

Confusingly, the second album (1969) had the same eponymous title as the first LP (in the States it was called *Man of Words/Man of Music*) but it was later re-titled on some editions *Space Oddity*. It would have made far more sense to give it that title from the get-go. Not that anything on the album bears any resemblance to that famous, intriguing and successful single.

A Hit Single

'Space Oddity' was typical of Bowie in the way it latched on to a prevailing theme – in this case excitement over the imminent moon landings – simply in order to subvert it. Few else in the euphoria of Neil Armstrong's giant leap for mankind would have dared make a haunting horror story of the proceedings by depicting an erratic astronaut condemning himself to a lonely death in the chilly depths of space. It became a UK No. 5.

With *The Man Who Sold The World* (1971), feyness finally drained from Bowie's music. This was doomy metal that sounded as though it had been forged somewhere not too distant from Black Sabbath's foundry. The cover shot was the opposite to such robustness, featuring a long-haired Bowie reclining, wearing a woman's dress. The highlight was the mysterious, sure-footed title track which, just to drive home the breadth of his talents, was decorated with his own snaking saxophone work.

THE MAN FROM MARS

'I DON'T THINK ALADDIN SANE IS AS CLEAR CUT AND DEFINED A CHARACTER AS ZIGGY WAS.'
DAVID BOWIE

Some fairly prestigious sessioners had worked on the second album but, with *The Man Who Sold the World*, Bowie had started assembling a band that would form the nucleus of his accompaniment for several years. Mick Ronson – brilliant guitarist, fine pianist, musical arranger, partner in his production team and even, it has been suggested, sometimes unacknowledged co-writer – was the principal one, while bassist Trevor Bolder and drummer Mick 'Woody' Woodmansey were the others.

From 1971 to 1973 Bowie would, with their aid, produce a trio of albums that for many are both his finest moments and high watermarks in recorded music per se.

'I WASN'T SURPRISED THAT ZIGGY STARDUST MADE MY CAREER. I PACKAGED A TOTALLY CREDIBLE PLASTIC ROCK STAR.'

DAVID BOWIE

Aptly Named *Hunky Dory*

In some ways the most extraordinary among them is *Hunky Dory*, partly because it appeared only eight months after its predecessor but mostly because this colossal masterpiece was thrown together by Bowie to pacify a record company hungry for product while he was laying the groundwork for his intended but time-consuming magnum opus. Would any other artist record a stop-gap packed to the gills with such melodic and lyrical inspiration as the dread-laced 'Changes', the phantasmagorical 'Life on Mars?', the haunting 'Quicksand' and the touching tribute to his troubled sibling 'The Bewlay Brothers'?

Ziggy Played ... Glam Rock

Bowie, though, had not just artistic excellence on his mind but superstardom. Accordingly, he cropped his hair, dyed it red and unleashed that magnum opus under the mouthful of a title *The Rise and Fall of Ziggy Stardust and The Spiders From Mars*. The album's concept was as illusory as that of The Beatles' *Sgt. Pepper* (1967) had been: only four of the 11 tracks could plausibly be said to be about the titular alien rocker. It didn't seem to matter: Bowie's unprecedentedly eerie make-up and outlandish costumes helped to create a public willingness to go along with the conceit. Outstanding songs like 'Five Years' (a moving requiem for a dying planet Earth), the soaring 'Starman' and the bitchy hard rock of 'Ziggy Stardust' didn't harm the cause either.

Bowie became bracketed with the proponents of glam rock – a genre that had more to do with dandyism than a musical style, yet was also somehow able to encompass the leather-clad likes of Suzi Quatro and Alvin Stardust. Bowie, though, took its androgyny a stage further: in January 1972 he stated that he was gay (despite being known to be married and a father). Record-buying youth initially responded with the same revulsion as their parents but then performed a somersault when they gleefully realized that being a fan of Bowie was something with which they could shock their elders.

Building On Success

'Starman' rescued Bowie from one-hit-wonder status; the *Ziggy* album remained in the UK chart for over 100 weeks and Bowie had become the most novel rock star for half a decade.

Aladdin Sane was the consolidation album. Neither as sweeping as *Hunky Dory* nor as seismic as *Ziggy*, it was still boundary-pushing – from its bizarre what does he-look-like cover photo to lyrics studded with words like 'wanking' and 'whore', it confirmed that Bowie was a new breed: too flash to be a rock star, too adult to be a pop star. As usual these days, Bowie's music was superb, with the pile-driving 'The Jean Genie' providing the hit and the achingly tender, spectral 'Lady Grinning Soul' becoming the track to which people pointed to prove there was no one else like him.

'FUNNILY ENOUGH, AND YOU'LL NEVER BELIEVE ME, IT WAS A PARODY OF GABRIEL ROSSETTI. SLIGHTLY ASKEW, OBVIOUSLY.'

DAVID BOWIE ON THE HUNKY DORY COVER

REBEL
REBEL

'IT'S THE FIRST RECORD I'VE ACTUALLY LIKED SINCE HUNKY DORY.' DAVID BOWIE ON YOUNG AMERICANS

'IT'S THE FIRST RECORD I'VE ACTUALLY LIKED SINCE HUNKY DORY.'
DAVID BOWIE ON YOUNG AMERICANS

If fame is a test, Bowie failed it. The mid-Seventies saw him dispense with his backing musicians, compounding their low remuneration by not telling them in advance of his July 1973 stage announcement that this was the last Spiders from Mars gig. He descended into drug addiction that saw him rival The Rolling Stones' Keith Richards as the world's unhealthiest-looking man. He also became so consumed in a Messiah complex that in 1976 he felt able to make a glib public announcement that Britain was ready for a dose of fascism.

'SOMETIMES I DON'T FEEL AS IF I'M A PERSON AT ALL. I'M JUST A COLLECTION OF OTHER PEOPLE'S IDEAS.'

DAVID BOWIE

'I SUPPOSE I'VE BEEN KNOCKING ON HEAVEN'S DOOR FOR ABOUT ELEVEN YEARS NOW, WITH ONE SORT OF HIGH OR ANOTHER.'

DAVID BOWIE, 1976

A Pair Of Follies

At first, the music described the same downwards arc; *Pin Ups* (1973) and *Diamond Dogs* (1974) were both grand follies. In the former, Bowie gave his usual treatment (i.e. one wasn't sure if he was taking the mick) to a collection of covers of British beat group records that he had liked as a young musician. It was quite enjoyable, particularly No. 3 UK single 'Sorrow' – and the publishing royalties were no doubt keenly appreciated by the sometimes obscure musicians to whom they made their way – but it was an absolute non sequitur of a work. Concept album *Diamond Dogs* marked Bowie's adoption of author William Burroughs' 'cut-up' technique – randomly reassembling severed lines of lyric – that he has used intermittently since. This album was as ambitious as *Pin Ups* was purposeless. It showed, however, that his old workmanlike Spiders rhythm section could trump the top sessioners to whom Bowie had returned, while his own lead guitar was not in the same league as the departed Mick Ronson's. Moreover, the songs were unexceptional apart from the anthemic '1984' and 'Rebel Rebel'. The latter was an irresistible stomping Stones clone that kept up his string of smash hits.

Turning A Corner

Although his behaviour remained erratic, Bowie was able to sort out his art. He turned to what he was happy to call 'plastic soul', particularly appropriate for an artist who always seemed to be saying 'but-not-really'. Some bridled at the cynicism of

'THE RIFF CAME FROM CARLOS AND THE MELODY AND MOST OF THE LYRICS CAME FROM ME, BUT IT WOULDN'T HAVE HAPPENED IF JOHN HADN'T BEEN THERE.'

DAVID BOWIE ON WRITING 'FAME'

co-opting a form of black music for his own amusement and careerist ends but it certainly saved him from the vortex when the glam movement with which he was associated went down the plughole of history.

As was almost always the case with Bowie, there was also no denying the power of the music. Some thought the songs overlong, some a little soporific, but the title track was slinky; 'Fascination' was unspeakably funky and the percolating 'Fame' – co-written with John Lennon and Carlos Alomar – even won over the hitherto Bowie-sceptic Americans, becoming his first No. 1 in that country.

If Bowie was caused anxiety by the fact that the two *Young Americans* singles barely scraped into the UK Top 20, he needn't have been: that same year a reissued 'Space Oddity' bizarrely became his first UK No. 1.

Yet Another Transformation

Those who assumed that *Young Americans* heralded a long-term new direction for Bowie were disabused of that by 1976 follow-up *Station to Station*. Its music was perfectly in keeping with his role as an odd-duck extra-terrestrial in *The Man Who Fell To Earth* (1976): stately and distant, although not without tenderness. It was also often very good. Although of standard album length, there were just six songs. The opening title cut was audaciously over 10 minutes long. However audacious Bowie was, though, he retained an innate populism: the glittering 'Golden Years' became a UK and US top tenner.

SCREEN STAR

'I DO SOME ACTING JOBS OCCASIONALLY, BUT I DON'T REALLY THINK IT'S A CAREER. IT'S SOMETHING THAT I GET OFFERED EVERY NOW AND AGAIN ...'
DAVID BOWIE

It's easy to mock rock stars who pursue parallel careers as thespians. Firstly, because said parallel career has usually only been opened to them by their 'proper' job and, secondly, because the presumption of thinking they can excel at something for which others often study for years is mildly contemptible.

Perhaps it's something to do with his early dramatic arts training under the tutelage of Lindsay Kemp but Bowie's acting career has bucked the trend of indulged rocker's self-delusion.

Loving The Alien

His entrée into the field was sort of obvious. Looking around for someone to play a stranded alien in *The Man Who Fell To Earth* (1976), director Nicolas Roeg plumped for someone who had, in a sense, already played an extra-terrestrial. Bowie proved all the doubters wrong, hiding his estuary accent and convincing audiences that he was a being not quite in synch with earthly ways. He was also comfortable in *Just a Gigolo* (1978) and *Christiane F* (1981).

In 1980, he took on the title role in a Broadway production of *The Elephant Man*. Impressively, he was convincing as the horribly deformed John Merrick without the benefit of prosthetics. It was a pointer to how this sex symbol's acting career would in no way be one that concentrated on roles in which he could purvey glamour.

An Opportune Brace

Part of the reason for the explosion in Bowie's fame in 1983 was the timing of the release of his album *Let's Dance* to coincide with two movies in which he made creditable performances. One was the claustrophobic prisoner of war movie *Merry Christmas, Mr. Lawrence*, while the other was a complete contrast. *The Hunger* was described by one noted film critic as 'kinky trash masquerading as a horror film', which might well be true but this tale of a man whose ageing is massively accelerated was also extremely watchable.

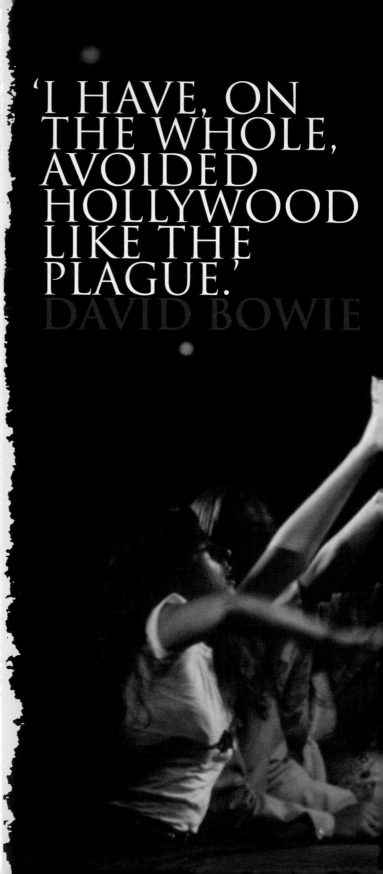

'I HAVE, ON THE WHOLE, AVOIDED HOLLYWOOD LIKE THE PLAGUE.'
DAVID BOWIE

'WE LOOKED
AROUND
EACH
OTHER
AND SAID
"THIS IS A
PILE OF
F*** SO
LET'S HAVE
A GOOD
TIME!"

DAVID
BOWIE ON
JUST A
GIGOLO

Bowie was only as good as the film itself in *Absolute Beginners* (1986), which is to say not very. It also began a tendency for him to contribute to the project's soundtrack – surely counter-productive to the idea of establishing his worth as an actor in his own right. He was a goblin king in Jim Henson's wonderful *Labyrinth* (also 1986) and if he was acted off the screen by Rob Mills, well, who could match the screen charisma of a seven-foot lovably lugubrious hairy monster? Having said that, the blush-making bulge in Bowie's tights had a good go.

Even his cameos were intriguing, for instance Pontius Pilate in *The Last Temptation of Christ* (1988) and an FBI agent in *Twin Peaks: Fire Walk with Me* (1992).

Bowie's role as mad scientist Nikola Tesla in *The Prestige* (2006) was also betwixt and between cameo and lead but again he put in a performance that, if not show-stealing, was highly impressive.

Greatest Performance

Possibly Bowie's most impressive film role of all was in *Basquiat* (1996). This biopic was of an artist of dubious talent who didn't even lead a particularly interesting life before his premature death. Bowie, though, was the best thing in the picture as Andy Warhol: another artist of dubious talent who comes into the title character's orbit. Bowie had written a song back on *Hunky Dory* about how tickled he was by the painter of Campbell's soup cans but that was no reason why he would be utterly convincing playing this fey, sexless and quintessentially American man.

'I DON'T KNOW WHETHER I'M AN ACTOR OR NOT, AND I WON'T KNOW UNTIL I SEE THE MOVIE IN A CINEMA WITH PEOPLE AROUND ME.'

DAVID BOWIE ON THE MAN WHO FELL TO EARTH

HIGH TO LOW

'I WAS
DISAPPOINTED
IN THE
RECEPTION
LOW GOT
FROM THE
PRESS – I GAVE
THEM MORE
CREDIT THAN
THAT.'
DAVID BOWIE

In 1976 Bowie abandoned LA, where he had been living for the past couple of years, retreating to the musical backwaters of Berlin. He set about devising *Low*, an album that would become the first instalment of a trilogy so unlike anything by either him or any other artist that he seemed intent on making himself a rock 'n'roll suicide.

One thing it at least enabled was his riding out the New Wave currently cresting back in his home country. While fellow members of the rock aristocracy had to endure the wrath of punks for their decadence and recent artistic mediocrity, Bowie was immune – even if only because nobody knew what to make of him anymore.

'I DISCOVERED
HOW LITTLE
I KNEW,
HOW LITTLE
I HAVE TO
SAY. THE
LACK OF
LYRICS ON
LOW
REFLECTS
THAT I WAS
LITERALLY
STUCK FOR
WORDS.'

DAVID
BOWIE

The High Of *Low*

Low started as a proposed soundtrack to *The Man Who Fell To Earth* but was rejected by Nicolas Roeg as unsuitable. Bowie recruited ex-Roxy Music keyboardist Brian Eno to help him build on the tracks. The result was a mash-up of the angular, artificial and weird-noise-punctuated sounds common to the nascent electronica musical genre, and Bowie's usual melodic, arch pop. The first vinyl side comprised of shorter tracks, whereas the second was given over to four glacial, almost completely instrumental semi-epics.

Perhaps what is now called the Berlin Trilogy is not as confrontational as Bowie would like to have us think, as he made damn sure that all three of the albums had at least one tuneful cut of radio-friendly length. In this case it was the exquisite 'Sound and Vision', a track absolutely stuffed with instrumental and vocal hooks that became a UK No. 3. The cockneyfied, sweet-natured 'Be My Wife' would surely have done similar business had it also been released as a single.

We Could Be "Heroes"

Eno took a bigger role on *"Heroes"*, often writing the music and leaving Bowie to concentrate on the lyrics. The latter described Bowie's discovery of new hope after climbing out of the cocaine hell partly charted by the previous album's songwords. Stuff like the ambient, vocal-less 'Sense of Doubt' and 'Moss Garden' made no concessions to commerciality

but were still strangely compelling. The high-gloss, ultra-tuneful cut this time was the title track and it's rather surprising that Bowie's assertion that he and his lover could be "Heroes" – with quotation marks – just for one day could climb only as high as No. 24 in the UK.

The Third Instalment

Bowie completed the trilogy in 1979 with an album that had nothing to do with Berlin: *Lodger*. If parts of the previous album sounded like Brian Eno using Bowie as a Trojan horse to reach a mass market usually unavailable to him, *Lodger* saw Bowie swing a little back towards traditional pop structures and principles. Strangely, though, this didn't engender great sales, even if he scored a UK Top 10 with the preeningly anthemic 'Boys Keep Swinging'. Despite the pop, there was no disguising that some tracks like 'African Night Flight' continued to be sheer avant-garde.

When recording artists cite the Berlin Trilogy as their favourite of Bowie's works, one often gets the impression of pretension. Despite this, the Trilogy is all the things that are claimed for it: high quality, daring and never quite categorizable. No artist has ever struck out for such an extended period into territories he had no way of knowing wouldn't alienate his followers.

'I'M SO PLEASED THAT THE CONCLUSION OF THESE THREE ALBUMS HAS BEEN SO UP ... AT LEAST THIS ONE HAS A KIND OF OPTIMISM.'

DAVID BOWIE ON LODGER

WHO LOVES HIM?

'DAVID BOWIE IS EASILY THE MOST INFLUENTIAL AND IMPORTANT ARTIST TO COME OUT OF THE UK.'
JOHNNY MARR, THE SMITHS

In many ways, it's surprising that David Bowie has inspired other musicians.

An artist who sloughs off styles on a regular basis is by definition not one easy to imitate. Yes, it's possible to do a takeoff of that quivering, mannered, cockney-inflected Bowie vocal style but, whereas everyone knows what you mean if you talk of an archetypal Rolling Stones song, there is no instantly recognizable Bowie musical signature.

Commonly Spotted Bowie Fan

Yet it's not difficult to spot his fans. Whether it be Gary Numan, Echo and the Bunnymen, Joy Division, The Smiths/Morrissey, Suede or Pulp, something about their affected delivery, the esoteric subjects of their lyrics or the rejection of rockin' archetypes of their instrumentation marks them out as people who went to concerts in the Seventies with a lightning flash painted on their adolescent faces or who have spent many hours intently listening to the recorded Bowie *oeuvre*.

The Goon Squad

In some cases, the influence has been risible. The frilly shirts, trailing headbands, and powdered and rogued men of early Eighties New Romanticism – like glam, a movement without a sound – smacked of Bowie devotees finally being able to wear the clothes in emulation of their idol that their mums had forbidden them to when they were children. When movement lynchpin Steve Strange titled his club Helden – German for *heroes* – it somehow seemed telling that he left out the quotation marks that Bowie had placed around his song title. Then there was Bauhaus: Eighties Goths who seemed to think that draining their lyrics of any warmth and rendering their songs in a passionless monotone meant that they were just like Bowie but missing entirely the frequent love and humour in Bowie's songs. The nadir of this was their inexplicable decision to put out as a single a cover of 'Ziggy Stardust'.

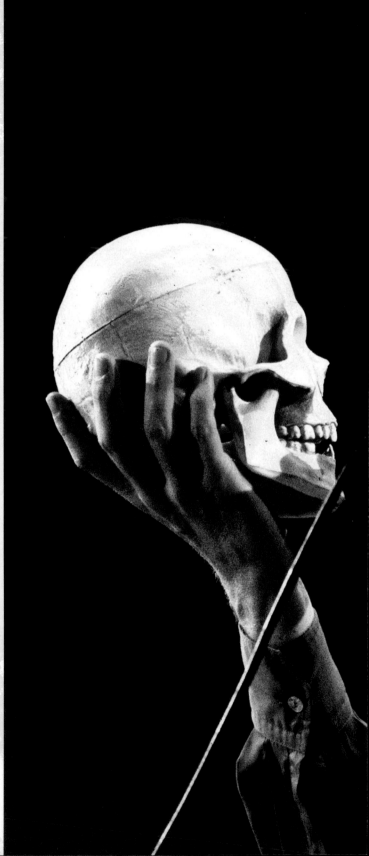

'LOW HAS ALWAYS BEEN MY FAVOURITE RECORD, AND EVEN MORE SO RECENTLY THE MORE I'VE LISTENED TO IT.'

However, there is far more to Bowie's influence than the above-named artists being inspired to pick up a guitar or sit down at a synthesizer. The fact that we live today in a knowing, quippy culture where the public are routinely tipped a wink by artists or advertisers – a shared acknowledgment of artifice – is something directly, if not exclusively, traceable to a pop star who pretended to be an alien, became a pop star and wrote the line: 'Don't think you knew you were in this song.'

Bowie's post-modern and chameleon tendencies have been evident in the actions of artists who have changed their image with every new release, from Adam Ant to Dexys Midnight Runners and Madonna to Lady Gaga.

The Most Crucial Impact

Perhaps Bowie's biggest pop legacy stems from that 'I'm gay' quote. He later called it the biggest mistake of his life because of the way it thwarted his career for a long time in puritanical America, but it gave many homosexual musicians the courage to come out of the closet, starting with members of early Eighties bands like Bronski Beat, Culture Club and Frankie Goes to Hollywood. It has now reached a point where it is so common that it's hardly even noteworthy for a gay musician to be upfront about his sexual identity. Ironically, it may have all been another piece of self-publicity, as Bowie's life has clearly been exclusively hetero for several decades and his historic male lovers seem to be the stuff only of rumour.

'I LOOK AT BOWIE AS AN ICON IN ART. IT'S NOT JUST ABOUT THE MUSIC. IT'S ABOUT THE PERFORMANCE, THE ATTITUDE, THE LOOK; IT'S EVERYTHING.'

LADY GAGA

OUT OF
THE ASHES

'IT'S VERY
MUCH A 1980s
NURSERY
RHYME.'
DAVID BOWIE
ON 'ASHES
TO ASHES'

I n 1979 Bowie had a non-album UK Top 10 hit with 'John I'm Only Dancing (Again)', a song that – the old rascal – bore no relation to his 1972 non-album No. 12 hit 'John I'm Only Dancing'.

A Homeland No. 1 At Last

The following year saw him gain his first UK No. 1 single that wasn't a reissue. 'Ashes to Ashes' was a haunting sequel to 'Space Oddity' (coincidentally, his only previous chart topper) that suggested there were narcotics-related reasons for Major Tom's space meltdown. The fact that the surreal video for the record – Bowie eerily playing pantomime character Pierrot – was the most expensive yet made seems now an indication of his apprehension that the MTV age was coming.

The Mainstream – Sort Of

The record's parent album *Scary Monsters (and Super Creeps)* (1980) continued Bowie's incremental return to the mainstream – or what, with him, passed for it. Yes, 'Up the Hill Backwards' had an instantly catchy melody but what did it actually mean? And surely most of the album's guitars are out of tune? However, who could resist the likes of 'Fashion'? This syncopated mocking of contemporary clothes horses was a UK No. 5 and the second of the album's four Top 40 UK singles. This was all capped by 'Under Pressure' – his collaboration with Queen – climbing to No. 1 in the UK (No. 29 in the States).

Nobody could have predicted that this triumph heralded an abandonment of musical adventurism and an aesthetic nadir.

When Bowie had a UK Top 3 with Bing Crosby in the shape of 'Peace On Earth/Little Drummer Boy' in late 1982 – a legacy of a bizarre 1977 guest appearance on the old crooner's TV show – his fans naturally dismissed it as much of an aberration as 'The Laughing Gnome', which belatedly made No. 6 in the UK in 1973. If only.

The man who had publicly said in 1976, 'I really, honestly and truly, don't know how much longer my albums will sell … And I really don't give a s***' now set about a cynical grab for the big time.

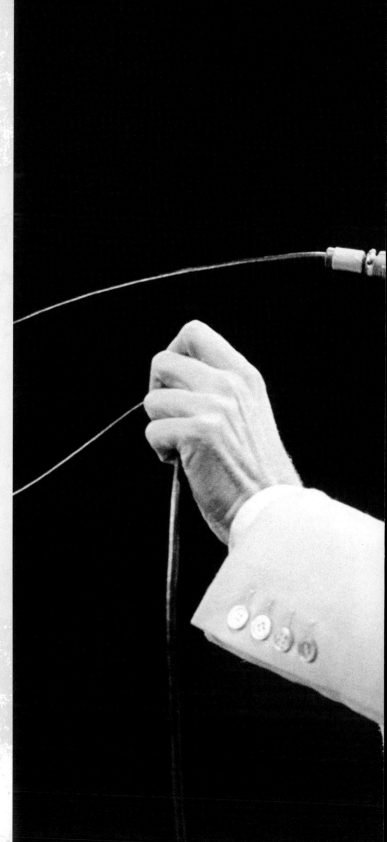

'THERE, IN THE CHORDS AND MELODIES, IS EVERYTHING I WANT TO SAY. THE WORDS JUST JOLLY IT ALONG.'

He brutally dispensed with the services of long-term producer Tony Visconti and turned to the in-vogue and very mainstream Nile Rodgers, Chic's main man. Maybe Bowie felt obliged to do well for EMI America following his megabucks switch from RCA – $17.5 million dollars was a lot of money in those days.

Superstardom At A Price

The resultant album, released in 1983, was called *Let's Dance*. More than a third of its eight songs weren't even new: Bowie had co-written 'China Girl' a few years back for an Iggy Pop album, 'Cat People' was a re-recording of a soundtrack song that had been a minor hit for him the previous year and 'Criminal World' was a cover. Moreover, with the exception of the mildly experimental 'Ricochet', much of the new material skirted a generic quality never previously perpetrated by this artist.

And the upshot? Almost by force of will, it seemed, Bowie turned from a middle ranker into a superstar. The thunderous but empty title track was a US No. 1 and the first of three UK Top 3 singles the album bequeathed. Bowie finally broke America properly, his Serious Moonlight Tour pulling in crowds who had never even heard of Ziggy Stardust.

'IT WAS GREAT IN ITS WAY, BUT IT PUT ME IN A REAL CORNER IN THAT IT F***KED WITH MY INTEGRITY.'

DAVID BOWIE ON LET'S DANCE

ROCK'N' ROLL SUICIDE

'I ENJOYED THE HELL OUT OF IT ... THE FACT THAT I COULD STILL CAUSE THAT AMOUNT OF HOSTILITY.'
DAVID BOWIE ON TIN MACHINE

Bowie's mega-success with his artistic low point was followed by what can only be described as a lost decade.

He followed up *Let's Dance* with the flimsy *Tonight* in 1984. Recorded straight after the Serious Moonlight Tour, it contained only two songs written by Bowie alone. While the seven-minute 'Loving The Alien' was in Bowie songs' noble questing tradition and the transatlantic Top 10 hit 'Blue Jean' could be, in the right mood, enjoyable, the fact that he had to resort to resurrecting old collaborations with Iggy Pop and covering Beach Boys and Leiber–Stoller songs to make up the numbers begged the question of why he had bothered releasing the thing in the first place.

Confused Artist

Bowie didn't even seem to know himself, judging by comments he made in interviews. A clue might be provided by the fact that Tina Turner was a guest vocalist on the reggaefied title track; perhaps he now regarded himself in the same middle-of-the-road bracket as the R&B chanteuse, lately restyled as a multi-platinum chart act.

Bowie busied himself with acting roles (usually involving accompanying soundtrack work) for the next few years. His 1985 UK No. 1 with Mick Jagger off the back of Live Aid 'Dancing in the Street' and his UK no. 2 'Absolute Beginners' – title theme for the movie – gave an illusion of continued viability during this period, but his next album *Never Let Me Down* (1987) spawned no Top 20 hits either side of the Atlantic. The record at least found Bowie writing again and one track – 'Time Will Crawl' – would have been excellent if it weren't for the cacophonous drum sound. However, neither the rest of the album nor its over-theatrical accompanying tour bespoke an inspired artist.

Tin Ear

There then followed a period that seemed to be marked by a loss of confidence and a desire for disappearance – as far as such is possible for a superstar – verging on self-loathing. Bowie announced that his days as a solo artist were over and that from now on he would merely be part of a band: the hard rock Tin Machine. Tin Machine didn't have any big hits, but

'I FEEL, ON THE WHOLE, FAIRLY HAPPY... I GUESS I WANTED TO PUT MY MUSICAL THING IN A SIMILAR STAID AND HEALTHY AREA.'

that wasn't the point of a band like this. If the point, however, was artistic credibility, it was a failure: Tin Machine's two studio albums (1989 and 1991) were deafeningly mediocre and painfully self-conscious. A live performance on the BBC's *Wogan* show in 1991 to publicize *Tin Machine II* was embarrassing; a pub band would have been booed off the stage for coming out with such a racket.

Personal Happiness At Least

In the middle of all this came his solo tour Sound+Vision. This might on the surface seem a good thing but there was self-negation involved even in a jaunt playing his widely loved oldies, as he declared that after this he would never be performing them again.

Bowie at least found the validation in his personal life that he apparently couldn't in his art. His first marriage to Angela Bowie had ended in 1980 after bequeathing a son Zowie (the subject of his song 'Kooks'), who is now better known as film director Duncan Jones. In 1990 Bowie met and fell head over heels in love with Somalian supermodel Iman, whom he married in 1992.

'I WAS SOMETHING I NEVER WANTED TO BE. I WAS A WELL-ACCEPTED ARTIST. I HAD STARTED APPEALING TO PEOPLE WHO BOUGHT PHIL COLLINS' ALBUMS.'

DAVID BOWIE

LOOKING FOR DIRECTION

'MY FAVOURITE
[ALBUM] IS STILL
BUDDHA OF
SUBURBIA.
I REALLY FELT
HAPPY MAKING
THAT ALBUM.'
DAVID BOWIE,
2003

Bowie proceeded to renege on both his declaration that he would never record outside Tin Machine and, in time, his assertion that he would not play his old hits for live audiences. Nobody seemed inclined to sue him for breach of promise.

The fact that he once again engaged the production services of Nile Rodgers hardly boded well for *Black Tie White Noise* (1993). Mercifully, though, this was no *Let's Dance*. How weird and/or apposite that Rodgers should help pull Bowie from the decade-long slump that he had helped to precipitate.

Newly Inspired

The record was as engaged and adventurous as *Let's Dance* was aimless and conservative, and only the irritatingly brittle drums spoiled the proceedings. The album found Bowie in cheerful mood, a clue to which would seem to be the fact that the opening and closing tracks were about his nuptials. He delved into his jazz hinterland like never before, as well as exploring the more modern sound of club techno. The album contained three instrumentals, one of which – 'Looking For Lester' – saw Bowie duel on sax with trumpeter Lester Bowie (no relation). There were several covers but, unlike *Let's Dance* and *Tonight,* they were intriguing rather than bewildering (e.g. a Morrissey song that had sampled his own 'Rock 'n' Roll Suicide'). The drunkenly tuneful 'Jump They Say' became a UK Top 10.

In the same year came *The Buddha of Suburbia*. The fact that even a Bowie soundtrack album had gravitas proved he was on an upswing, although it should be conceded that this was not a conventional soundtrack, as Bowie played fast and loose with the score he had originally provided the BBC for their dramatization of Hanif Kureishi's novel. Arista allocated the album the same promotional budget as any other soundtrack, thus probably accounting for the fact that the wistful title track climbed no higher than No. 35 in the UK. In any event, Bowie was, like many 'heritage' artists, moving beyond a point where singles particularly mattered.

More Drama Than Music

The bizarrely titled *1. Outside* (1995) saw Bowie reunite with another former producer, Brian Eno, for what was surely his most ambitious work ever. Far more like a radio play than an album, it was a grisly narrative – complete with spoken-word sections and oodles of sound effects – about the investigation into how a teenage girl's insides came to be used as an art exhibit. The fact that Bowie attempted free-form jazz, jungle and techno was a little disconcerting: he used to set the trend, not follow it. Moreover, almost all the songs were co-written with his producer and/or colleagues. Even so, tracks like 'Segue: Baby Grace (A Horrid Cassette)' and 'Wishful Beginnings' were disquietingly compelling.

Embracing The Modern

Earthling (1997) saw Bowie crank up the tilt at relevance by experimenting with jungle/drum and bass, industrial rock and techno. 'Urgh!' must have been the response of some of his now primarily middle-aged fanbase. It was certainly more courageously contemporary than it was listenable, with the quiet parts of 'Seven Years in Tibet' the only relief from jungle's merciless industrial tone.

Another 'Urgh!' moment for some was the announcement of 'Bowie Bonds', whereby Bowie took advantage of the new concept of forfeiting to investors projected royalties in exchange for immediate cash. Despite the disgust, it was a canny move; it was as if he'd seen that the internet would shortly decimate the mechanical royalties revenue stream.

'BLACK TIE WHITE NOISE REFERS TO THE VERY OBVIOUS – THE RADICAL BOUNDARIES THAT HAVE BEEN PUT UP IN MOST OF THE WESTERN WORLD.'

'I LOVE BEING EXCITED BY WHAT I DO. I'M STILL PLAYING EARTHLING EVERY DAY. I'VE NOT STOPPED ENJOYING IT.'

DAVID BOWIE

OH! YOU PRETTY THING

'WHAT BECAME KNOWN AS GLAM OR GLITTER ROCK WASN'T A MOVEMENT AT ALL, MUSICALLY. IT WAS VERY LIMITED.'
DAVID BOWIE

In March 2013 it was announced that 'David Bowie is' – an exhibition at London's Victoria and Albert Museum – had become the fastest-selling in the institution's history. The traditionally minded V&A had clearly cottoned on to the fact that Bowie, more than any music icon, enabled them to fulfil their remit of exploring art and design in the culture.

Chameleon Cliché

The fact that the description of Bowie as style chameleon is a groan-inducing cliché does not make it untrue. Everyone from Madonna to Boy George to Lady Gaga has copied his propensity to use his own body as a canvas and to make that propensity – for better or worse – almost as important as the music.

'I ONCE ASKED LENNON WHAT HE THOUGHT OF WHAT I DO. HE SAID "IT'S GREAT, BUT IT'S JUST ROCK AND ROLL WITH LIPSTICK ON."'

DAVID BOWIE

Bowie was a dandy way back. Footage exists of him as a seventeen-year-old mod speaking up for the rights of long-haired males. Although he has a twinkle in his eye, his immaculately coiffured, sharp-suited look communicates that this is someone who takes his appearance very seriously.

By the time of *Hunky Dory*, Bowie was a long-haired hippie. However, an interplanetary gender-bending rocker could not step from his gleaming starship with locks tucked carelessly behind ears framing a pimpled face. For the next couple of years, Bowie sported short, dazzlingly red hair, make-up-cum-cosmic war paint, stack heels and sometimes an eyepatch. Although he outgrew that image, he would never go back to laid-back scruffiness.

Cover Jobs

Album cover artwork was intrinsic to his now ever-changing appearance. On *Aladdin Sane* he had a red-and-blue lightning flash across his face and a weird droplet – of what you tried to convince yourself wasn't semen – residing over a clavicle. On the wraparound cover of *Diamond Dogs*, he seemed to be trying to prove that he was the veritable dog's bollocks; the Guy Peellaert painting that gave him a man's upper body and a canine lower half originally had a penis and testicles, although that was quickly amended.

'ONCE YOU LOSE THAT SENSE OF WONDER AT BEING ALIVE, YOU'RE PRETTY MUCH ON THE WAY OUT...'

In order to purvey the soul of *Young Americans*, he remained stylish but more grown-up, striding around in baggy trousers and waistcoats – a masculinity offset by the fact that his now side-parted hair was fluffily arranged in a way that was not yet common with men. The Thin White Duke figure associated with *Station to Station* boasted slicked-back hair, a formal waistcoat but casual open collar and a cigarette dangling from the lips. Thankfully less easy for Bowie's admirers to imitate was the cokehead's telltale vacant manner and chalk-white skin tone.

Bowie kept appearances up even as his art was in the pits. Promoting and touring *Let's Dance*, he looked a million dollars with his slick blonde quiff and natty suits. Nor did he and his black-suited Tin Machine colleagues exactly dress shabbily.

Old But Gold

Although Bowie has never run to fat or gone bald, using his body as a canvas became more difficult with age as a natural function of the fact that the world's attention gravitates to younger clothes horses. Nonetheless, Bowie has continued to devise striking imagery: standing in a Union Jack coat while imperiously surveying England on the front of *Earthling* seemed designed to stake a (plausible) claim to be the instigator of the spirit behind Cool Britannia. His waxen face and milky eyes on *Heathen* (2002) were simply unnerving.

Pensioner he may now be, but it is unlikely that David Bowie will ever step into a camera lens's frame looking less than immaculate.

REALITY
CHECK

'IT'S SORT OF
PIONEERING
AND IT'S NOT
AN ACCEPTABLE
WAY TO GO.
AND THAT I
ALWAYS FIND
SUBVERSIVE
ENOUGH.'
DAVID BOWIE
ON 'BOWIE
BONDS'

Hours… (1999) saw Bowie co-writing with Tin Machine guitarist and subsequent frequent collaborator Reeves Gabrels.

The album had originated in a commission to score a computer game called *Omikron: The Nomad Soul*. One of the cuts, 'What's Really Happening', featured the credit of one Alex Grant, winner of an internet competition to write a lyric to a Bowie melody. Leaving that gimmick aside, the album was less self-consciously experimental than the previous two.

The music was generally warm, even if the lyrics were bad-tempered. The preponderance of mid-tempo and lengthy tracks gave the impression of songs serving the words but that's okay, even if the soothing 'Thursday's Child' and the snarling hard rock of 'The Pretty Things Are Going to Hell' are the only tracks that suggest a rock giant taking a time-out.

'STRANGELY ENOUGH, YOU DON'T ALWAYS WRITE WHAT YOU WANT TO WRITE.'

DAVID BOWIE ON WRITING SUNDAY

'THERE ARE NO YEARNING AMBITIONS ANY MORE … I HAVE A SENSE THAT I'VE BECOME THE PERSON THAT I ALWAYS SHOULD HAVE BEEN.'

DAVID BOWIE, 2002

The Lost Album

Heathen was the first album on Bowie's own ISO label, whose formation, rumour has it, was his response to previous label Virgin failing to release an album titled *Toy*. Both Bowie and Visconti had worked on it, mixing new songs with rearrangements of some of his oldies. Some of *Toy*'s tracks appeared as Bowie B-sides before the whole thing eventually found its way on to the internet. When it did, the consensus was that it was not a Beach Boys' *Smile*-type lost classic.

The Return Of Visconti

Heathen saw Bowie formally reunited with Tony Visconti for the first time since *Scary Monsters* nearly a quarter of a century before. Mixed discretely in with the conventional songcraft were modern techniques and styles. The title of its track 'Slow Burn' could be said to sum up the charms of an album of leisurely songs flecked with discrete decoration, although the poppy 'Everyone Says "Hi"' showed that his knack of creating an immediately hummable tune remained intact.

Reality (2003) was also pretty good, By now, Bowie's audience was so knowledgeable as to be able to respond to sonic shorthand; the album's haunting seven-minute closer 'Bring Me The Disco King' felt agreeably like a sequel to the title track of *Aladdin Sane* – right down to Mike Garson revisiting his fractured piano style from that recording.

Although sales of Bowie's albums had fluctuated in recent years and free-fallen in America, the fact that A Reality grossed more than any other tour that year showed where the big bucks were: for beloved artists with a substantial back catalogue

Retreating From View

When Bowie hit 50 in 1997, he had been publicly cheerful, telling one interviewer, 'It's incredible. I'm bouncy.' This must have come back to haunt him in mid-2004, when this preternaturally youthful-looking man suffered a heart attack. It caused the cancellation of the final dates of his A Reality Tour, which had already seen misfortune when a lollipop thrown by an audience member hit Bowie – shades of George Underwood – in the eye.

The whole situation seemed to unnerve Bowie, whose recent artistic energy suddenly evaporated. A man of Bowie's fame – and ego – can never disappear off the face of the earth, especially in the age of the internet, but he now battened down the hatches, restricting public appearances to such things as collecting his Lifetime Achievement Grammy in 2006, and cameos on friends' releases and concerts. On the few occasions when he spoke to the media during this period, he stated that he was perfectly happy being a stay-at-home dad to his daughter Alexandria, born in 2000.

WHERE ARE WE NOW?

"PEOPLE HAVE ASKED WHAT I'VE BEEN WORKING ON AND I'VE SAID "I CAN'T TELL YOU ... A MYSTERY PROJECT ... PROJECT X""

TONY VISCONTI ON THE NEXT DAY

On 8 January 2013 – his 66th birthday – Bowie not only broke his decade-long radio silence with the single 'Where Are We Now?' but also announced on his website that it was the precursor to a new full-length album that had been recorded in total secrecy over a two-year period.

Toying With The Media

Playing his usual cat-and-mouse games, Bowie announced that album producer Tony Visconti would henceforth be his representative with the press and that there would be no tour. Bowie also sent the *New Musical Express* a photograph of himself with the message: 'David would like to be on the cover.' The *NME* obliged – even though the guy in the picture

wore a featureless mask. (The uniquely contrasting eyes glittering through the eyeholes was the giveaway.)

Dubious Single, Good Album

The dirge-like 'Where Are We Now?' was actually one of the album's least impressive tracks (a recurring complaint about Bowie's choice of singles in recent years), even though it was intriguingly studded with references to his late Seventies residency in Berlin. Bowie had been self-referential on some of his recent albums but never so blatantly as on *The Next Day*, whose sleeve featured the front of "Heroes" with the title crossed out and the look-at-my-quiff photo obscured by the new album's name. Bowie scholars will no doubt debate the meaning of this for years to come. The music was reminiscent not of the Berlin Trilogy but of the fractured, tormented rock of *Scary Monsters*. The tunes were good and the lyrics as deliciously unenlightening as ever; there were a satisfactory number of weird sound effects and a pleasing overall variety of tone. It was a UK No. 1 and a career-high US No. 2.

With perfect timing for this air of new relevance, in May 2013 astronaut and part-time musician Chris Hadfield posted online from the International Space Station a video of himself performing 'Space Oddity' in zero gravity. A tickled Bowie tweeted his approval.

This all leaves the question handily posed for us by the artist: where are we now?

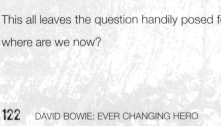

'WOULD BE LOVELY IF ALL OF YOU WOULD SPREAD THE WORD ABOUT DA'S NEW ALBUM. FIRST IN TEN YEARS, AND IT'S A GOOD 'UN!'

Predictable Unpredictability

Some will suggest that it's difficult for a man heading towards his seventieth birthday to continue to command attention. Another decade-long silence might maintain his aura of myth but there's no guarantee he would even live to see the end of it.

However, we've been here before, numerous times. For instance, many were those in 1972 who would have snorted at the idea that an artist so obsessed with superficiality and chart success would sustain a multi-decade career characterized by career-jeopardising innovation.

It's another fact about Bowie that might be groan-inducing cliché but is nonetheless true: expect the unexpected.

FURTHER INFORMATION

DAVID BOWIE VITAL INFO

Birth Name	David Robert Jones
Birth Date	8 January 1947
Birth Place	London, England
Nationality	British
Height	1.78m (5 ft 10 in)
Hair Colour	Light Brown
Eye Colour	Blue/Brown
Alter Ego	David Bowie

DISCOGRAPHY

Albums

David Bowie (1967)

Space Oddity (1969)

The Man Who Sold The World (1970)

Hunky Dory (1971)

The Rise and Fall of Ziggy Stardust and The Spiders from Mars (1972)

Aladdin Sane (1973)

Pin Ups (1973)

Diamond Dogs (1974)

Young Americans (1975)

Station to Station (1976)

Low (1977)

"Heroes" (1977)

Lodger (1977)

Scary Monsters (and Super Creeps) (1980)

Let's Dance (1983)

Tonight (1984)

Never Let Me Down (1987)

Tin Machine (1989)

Tin Machine II (1991)

Black Tie White Noise (1993)

The Buddha of Suburbia (1993)

outside (1995)

Earthling (1997)

'Hours…' (1999)

Heathen (2002)

Reality (2003)

The Next Day (2013)

Selected Singles

1969: 'Space Oddity' (UK No. 1)

1972: 'Starman' (UK No. 10)

'The Jean Genie' (UK No. 2)

1973: 'Drive-In Saturday' (UK No. 3)

'Life on Mars' (UK No. 3)

'Sorrow' (UK No. 3)

1974: 'Rebel Rebel' (UK No. 5)

'Knock on Wood' (UK No. 10)

1975: 'Fame' (US No. 1)

'Golden Years' (UK No. 8, US No. 10)

1977: 'Sound and Vision' (UK No. 3)

1979: 'Boys Keep Swinging' (UK No. 7)

1980: 'Ashes to Ashes' (UK No. 1)

'Fashion' (UK No. 5)

1981: 'Under Pressure' (with Queen) (UK No. 1)

1982: 'Peace on Earth/Little Drummer Boy'
(with Bing Crosby) (UK No. 3)

1983: 'Let's Dance' (UK No. 1, US No. 1)

'China Girl' (UK No. 2, US No. 10)

'Modern Love' (UK No. 2)

1984: 'Blue Jean' (UK No. 6, US No. 8)

1985: 'Dancing in the Street' (UK No. 1, US No. 7)

1986: 'Absolute Beginners' (UK No. 2)

1992: 'Jump They Say' (UK No. 9)

1996: 'Hallo Spaceboy' (UK No. 12)

1997: 'Little Wonder' (UK No. 14)

1999: 'Thursday's Child' (UK No. 16)

2013: 'Where Are We Now?' (UK No. 6)

AWARDS

BRIT Awards

1984: Best British Male

1996: Outstanding Contribution to British Music

GQ Awards

2000: Most Stylish Man of the Year

Grammy Awards

1985: Best Video, Short Form *Jazzin' for Blue Jean*

2006: Lifetime Achievement Award

Ivor Novello Awards

1969: Special Award for Originality 'Space Oddity'

MTV Video Music Awards

1984: Best Male Video 'China Girl'

Video Vanguard Award

1986: Best Overall Performance in a Video
'Dancing in the Street'

MuchMusic Video Awards

1998: EyePopper Award 'I'm Afraid of Americans'

Q Awards

1995: *Q* Inspiration Award

Webby Awards

2007: Webby Lifetime Achievement

TOURS

Ziggy Stardust Tour: January 1972–July 1973; UK, North American and Japan

Diamond Dogs Tour: June-December 1974; North America

Isolar – 1976 Tour: February-May 1976; North America and Europe

Isolar II – The 1978 World Tour: March–December 1978; Worldwide

Serious Moonlight Tour: May–December 1983; Worldwide

Glass Spider Tour: May–November 1987; Worldwide

Sound+Vision Tour: March–September 1990; Worldwide

Outside Tour: March–September 1990; North America and Europe

Outside Summer Festivals Tour: June–July 1996; Japan, Russia and Iceland

Earthling Tour: June–November 1997; Europe, North America and South America

The Hours...Tour: October–December 1999; North America and Europe

Mini Tour: June 2000; North America and Europe

Heathen Tour: June–October 2002; North America and Europe

A Reality Tour: October 2003–July 2004; Worldwide

ONLINE

davidbowie.com: David Bowie's official website.

@DavidBowieReal: For all things from Bowie himself.

facebook.com/davidbowie: With over 4 million likes David Bowie's Facebook page has all the must know information about his latest musical releases.

BIOGRAPHIES

Sean Egan (Author)

Londoner Sean Egan has contributed to, among others, *Billboard*, *Book Collector*, *Classic Rock*, *Record Collector*, *Tennis World*, *Total Film*, *Uncut* and RollingStone.com. He has written or edited nineteen books, including works on The Beatles, Jimi Hendrix, The Rolling Stones, Coronation Street, Manchester United and Tarzan. His critically acclaimed novel *Sick of Being Me* was published in 2003, while *Don't Mess with the Best*, his 2008 collection of short stories, carried cover endorsements from Booker Prize winners Stanley Middleton and David Storey.

Malcolm Mackenzie (Foreword)

Malcolm Mackenzie is the editor of *We Love Pop*. He started as a professional pop fan writing for teen titles like *Top of the Pops*, *Bliss* and *TV Hits* before moving into the adult market working for *GQ*, *Glamour*, *Grazia*, *Attitude*, and newspapers such as *The Times*, *The Sunday Times*, *The Guardian* and *thelondonpaper* where he was Music Editor for three years before returning to the teen sector to launch *We Love Pop*.

PICTURE CREDITS